THINGS ON WHICH
I'VE STUMBLED

ALSO BY PETER COLE

POETRY
Rift
Hymns & Qualms
What Is Doubled: Poems 1981–1998

TRANSLATION
Selected Poems of Shmuel HaNagid
Selected Poems of Solomon Ibn Gabirol
Love & Selected Poems, by Aharon Shabtai
From Island to Island, by Harold Schimmel
Qasida, by Harold Schimmel
Never Mind: Twenty Poems and a Story, by Taha Muhammad
    Ali (with Yahya Hijazi and Gabriel Levin)
So What: New & Selected Poems, 1971–2005, by Taha
    Muhammad Ali (with Yahya Hijazi and Gabriel Levin)
The Heart is Katmandu, by Yoel Hoffmann
Collected Poems, by Avraham Ben Yitzhak
The Shunra and the Schmetterling, by Yoel Hoffmann
J'accuse, by Aharon Shabtai
*The Dream of the Poem: Hebrew Poetry from Muslim
    and Christian Spain, 950–1492*

OTHER
Hebrew Writers on Writing

THINGS ON WHICH
I'VE STUMBLED

PETER COLE

 A NEW DIRECTIONS BOOK

Grateful acknowledgment is due to the editors of the following journals and volumes where some of these poems were first published: *The Aldeburgh Poetry Paper, Alligatorzine, Conjunctions, Der Hammer, Narrative.com, The Nation, No, Poetry, Princeton Library Chronicle, Shearsman, Talisman,* and *Zeek.*

"Proverbial Drawing" was first printed by the Jerusalem Print Workshop as a collaboration with the artist Seth Altholz, whose drawings led to the poem.

"Things on Which I've Stumbled" was composed while working at the Taylor-Schechter Genizah Research Unit at Cambridge University. My thanks to Ben Outhwaite, Rebecca Jefferson, and the members of the Unit for taking me into their fold and granting me access to that extraordinary collection and all it evokes.

Cover art: Joel Shapiro, Woodcut, "5748" ©1987 Joel Shapiro/ARS, printed by Leslie Miller at The Grenfell Press.

Manufactured in the United States of America.
New Directions Books are printed on acid-free paper.
First published as a New Directions Paperbook (NDP1119) in 2008.
Published simultaneously in Canada by Penguin Books Canada Limited.

Library of Congress Cataloging-in-Publication Data
Cole, Peter, 1957–
Things on which I've stumbled / Peter Cole.
p. cm.
ISBN 978-0-8112-1803-0 (alk. paper)
I. Title.
PS3553.O47325T55 2008
811'.54—dc22

                    2008022975

New Directions Books are published for James Laughlin
by New Directions Publishing Corporation
80 Eighth Avenue, New York, NY 10011
www.ndpublishing.com

For Forrest Gander, graphing a faithful existence
&
Martin Earl, who knows how an angel works

CONTENTS

IV.

The word has meaning from the moment adoration is produced in this world, when a finite being stands before something which goes beyond him.
— Emmanuel Levinas

IMPROVISATION ON LINES BY ISAAC THE BLIND

Only by sucking, not by knowing,
can the subtle essence be conveyed—
sap of the word and the world's flowing

that raises the scent of the almond blossoming,
and yellows the bulbul in the olive's jade.
Only by sucking, not by knowing.

The grass and oxalis by the pines growing
are luminous in us—petal and blade—
as sap of the word and the world's flowing;

a flicker rising from embers glowing;
light trapped in the tree's sweet braid
of what it was sucking. Not by knowing

is the amber honey of persimmon drawn in.
An anemone piercing the clover persuades me—
sap of the word and the world is flowing

across separation, through wisdom's bestowing,
and in that persuasion choices are made:
But only by sucking, not by knowing
that sap of the word through the world is flowing.

I

THINGS ON WHICH I'VE STUMBLED

among the remains of the Cairo Geniza

Poetry and all that garbage,
    left in a pocket
        of the mind
        or a pair of pants,
            a robe,
or slipped inside a book—
        thought's *disjecta membra*—
a letter forgotten
(a recipe scribbled on its back)
a shopping list,
or bill once due,
        living's marginalia—

the rubble of what we've known was true . . .

*

In a crawl space over the prayer floor,
a storeroom perched on Coptic columns,
high in the wall of the women's gallery
(reached by ascent on a ladder only
and entered doubled over . . .)
where the legend's serpent, waiting, coils—
the words in darkness held to paper,
rags really,
        brought to light in dimness linger
as words do, as knowing is
not what's there but how we lift it
up with the winches of syntax and sense,
up in the eye of desire for linkage
of every sort, including chance—
pointing and leading through that sense,

like Keats's hand,
        reaching through the poem . . .

And in your innocence being borne——

—

With me for a moment, please . . .

—

all carried,
        into the air and on

and with all his desire brought me
and from within his heart he taught me
        my heart's secret
and so my . . . was raised,
and my eye has not grown dim

. . . was the badge
   of sense they wore
      on their sleeves
         almost thin;
      beauty limned
   in so many seams,
though not as gems,

but soundings within——

as his desire made me
sad before him

—

as in addition what is brought—

as in addiction what is brought—

for certain
              what depends
on the wise and
worth of those who vow . . .

a hand to dig
     and the ripening grain . . .

and the dove sent through the woods,

and what was ruined made wondrous again:

all of which was found
on a scrap-heap,
     in the darkness,
rising through the minds of men:

Two women (twins)
found the thread
and pulled it toward them:

The wise will seek
the ancients' wisdom . . .
and keep the sayings
     of renowned men,

and enter into the subtleties
        of parables,

and search out their hidden valencies,
     and marvels,

and let their secrets speak to them . . .

  —said the linen
  rags informed
  by iron gall,
    of oak and wine—

"Do not speak about the matter
            till tomorrow.
I will come
    to you tomorrow
        about 11 p.m.,
and talk over . . .
                with you
how to make the matter known . . ."

—

    . . . over what remains;

    so with a pact
  you came, and
  with a claim—
  and it was kept
  and then made plain.

—

As everything precious my eye has seen
in you came to fruition . . .

—

. . . and there's the badge, once again
      linking beginning and end

though flames were sent throughout the land
and all song and melody fled
the angels above us and below
with whom my heart had sped
turned now to mourning

—

... where his presence is

—

(across me a cloud

my soul and ...)

—

... the pomegranate
groves ...
                sun ...
and ... persimmon—
nard and saffron ...

II.
And so not just
   the names of God
      they sought to guard
from desecration
   but the forms
      composing them:
"Letters are things,
   not pictures of things"
     —Eric Gill,
who'd reach Jerusalem.

And from the refuse-heap before him:

Five fine covers—
   one gazelle's blood red,
   one a violet that's pure,
   one the color of musk,
the others sulfur yellow and silver . . .

and eight small carpets—please,
   my lord,
the red should be as red as can be,
the yellow and white should be exquisite . . .

the gold brocade is very pretty
but not what I wanted exactly—
   for it's white and blue,
     while I had in mind an onion color,
       an open hue—
     but the lead-gray robe is superb . . .

—

You also asked for head-scarves,
although you know what a nuisance that is—
    the souk's packed
     from dawn to dusk—
  it made me have a relapse, twice,
       but this is what I bought:

one black, with a white border
    (just as you ordered),
another azure with gold threads,
the others oak-green, cream, and red;

you asked, too, about the pearl
and the light-grayish honeydew—
    but these were mediocre,
      or over-priced,
and, I think, a waste of money . . .

thus the color-
    intoxication
that's spoken of:
the dyes extracted from nature
(brazilwood, indigo, saffron, and soot,
asparagus, kermes, and murex
mixed with mordants)
for yarn which
           was soaked in it—
transformed then on a loom—
fulled or thrown, beaten and pressed,
to make a soul or room complete
    with what their poets knew—

that beauty carried covers
more than just a flaw
    or seam in being
that lets us see

what's real,
but is itself a means
of conducting things concealed
that can't, by nature, be revealed—

thus its evocation,
its calling forth
    and lifting,
thus the rabbis' saying
a person should always be willing
to overpay for clothing,
    but not for drink and food—

thus the route
along which fabric flowed like poems

—

Or this trousseau:

Two anklets
and rimmed bracelets;
two bracelets adorned with pearls;
    four rings of gold;
two earrings adorned with pearls
    and two silver rings;

a chain of twenty-three
    amber beads,
marked by nine   golden beads—

the amber being partly apples
    and partly plums. . . .

A small silver jewel-box—

ornaments for
that journey into union

and what the bride
would become,

and what would be adorned

in the making of their world—

—

I also need, one Ehli wrote
to a friend along the Nile,
the collection of Ibn Khalfon's poems—
        either send it on
                and I will copy it out,
        or have it copied for me.
Please!
For someone borrowed . . .
        from me . . .
and took it with him
        to Yemen.

I implore you, don't forget
to do that for me,
no matter what . . .

—

remember . . . which is before you,
with love like . . . armed

—

I am not able to answer because—

says the poem——
    with hardness of heart . . .
and therefore the fruits of my actions
. . . and among the poor, soon
therefore the blood in me boils . . .
as over coals of broom

is what, for instance, was retrieved
and boils still——

in dimness lingering
    as words will

—

And the world which

And how could it raise . . .
and how could it please
and the days again . . .
and death . . .
and what do I have or need with . . .

—

Dimness but not darkness
dark that doesn't descend
lighting up the blackness

And the hidden stores
of forces arousing

—

The body with nothing to lean on
. . . over nothing a tent . . .

To grasp the train of his robes
. . . . in your bowing
. . . . before him

—

with joy in . . . life
. . . . the end of days

—

And in your being borne
over that ocean
you are very close to them . . .
their mouths will bear
*   witness for them*
and who would not go in fear?

—

And friends . . .
zeal for Zion, which——

III.
Not just the past ascending into
      the present of a given seeing,
but that present itself collapsing
      into the voices speaking to it—

so that current, mixing, becomes
      duration which one, mostly, lives:
neither the now of mystical focus
      nor the then of an ancient grudge,

but rather time itself conceived
      of as an electron cloud above us.

—

Racing although there's no one leaving
. . . an exit for him
and settling

. . . in the shadow of your wings,
            seeking refuge

—

to the upper reaches of . . .

To the *outer* reaches of
what we've known and not,
      and then beyond it
            to what's been
forgotten
and banked in soot
            and dust

—

And day unto day speaks

—

Hurrying now . . .

I was wrong and wandered after . . .
the haughty . . .

    that month my spirit . . .
for you and the darkness withdrew
and I decreed

. . . *my coming into the broken city*

       city adrift,
   Seféris said, of refugees

—

The princes descending and rising again . . .
The riders before you . . .
. . . *and so he leaped* . . .

Hear me, please:

echoing
into centuries

. . . *the learned among them*
   and those who . . .
in vain, and frauds
Their . . . *in truth he*

Cut off by worms and time—
as we will be,
                    and are

—

Hidden in dirt, a fire

Now and then a leader emerging
    only to be put down again

—

Clouds of tears raining for . . .
they have freed . . .
and I'm astounded

—

And now my dove is gone
    from within her home,
        she fled while I was sleeping
            and lies now in a grave

So waves of what was breath
wash across the skin—
    not just vellum,
    but living—
as movement is
our lives' translation . . .

And then they rose against me
    and spread a net to trap me,
though I will sing out still
    extolling those who've raised me—

rendering the sweetest
song for he who watches me
and saves my soul from Hell
and the rest of me from ruin.

—

Thus the poet responds
                to cruelty
song the product of exigency
as it should be—but,
and this is what surprises,
    of loyalty
to what made him
what he was,
                and would be,
anger not his destiny . . .

And yet it's not that easy
is it

. . . *in my shame*

taking my desire to . . .
. . . . *complaint*

which is exasperation's petition
opening onto contrition

The soul in its frame . . .
                keeping its watches
. . . .

And seeking for their sadness one
to count the stars and names for all

IV.
Garbage is
             what isn't wanted,
     what's no longer *put to use*
and worthless in a certain eye—
     old amulets, and bills of lading,
pledges, contracts, i.o.u.'s—
     the weakened pages of fading hymns
or poems that meant the world to someone
     once—
             copied out then shipped
with silk and cloves
                       across The Sea—
     tossed now
             onto the scrap-heap,
longing's junkyard,
             a worm's feast,
     not quite given up entirely
but forgotten
             in a morgue
for speech that was
             committed to matter,
     staining it, and said to be
given by God—preserved,
                       like bodies,
brought back from their dormancy . . .

—

To you they . . .
. . . .
who have done their will
while a wretched people . . .

—

And he will not ascend unto
the heights of the altars so
as not to reveal . . .

—

Not to reveal *what?*

Why is aspiration shame,
Why is desire for deepest connection
    a source of abjection?

Because it betrays a lack of acceptance?

—

And drink the wine of my love
with me in my home

says the song
which lingers on

and shows no lack of longing.

—

But is that aspiration

To moisten the face of the world
. . . beads of dew for softness . . .

By your holy name, Lord, help me now
    and if I've erred, show me how to . . .

V.
These are things on which I've stumbled:

> *Those on high are distant voices*
> *   far away, on earth, calling*
> *from the depths increase your . . . skies*
> *. . .*

> *before he turns . . .*

> *. . . drew near you in your love and came*

the making of miracles such as forgiveness,
friendship souring inside aloneness,

delight which leaves one exalted and humbled,

> *I will give my single share,*
> *. . . . . . said the rag*
> *a rose cheek*
> *and breasts . . . .*

before the mind of another man.

These are things I could not fathom,

> *. . . . . . . your sons*
> *. . . . . your ways*
> *. . . . . . your kings*
> *. . . . . your . . .*

> *Plunders of a people*
> *. . . . . in darkness*

standing among them before I'd fallen—
hurting myself and others upon them:

>*How fine it is for a man of twenty*
>*fleet of foot . . . . Over the hills*
>*. . . . . chasing*
>*And then at thirty . . . .*
>*. . . . .*

>*And at forty . . .*

>*At fifty, suddenly,*
>*it all seems like*

>*one long elegy . . .*

lines of a poem that would lead to

>*Smoothly singing their words in*
>>*order*
>>>*to understand . . .*

the creation of truth through deception and fiction

>*against the voice that hardens*
>>*his heart to matters of love*
>*in seeing the rule of years*
>>*and the stars of . . .*
>*. . . . .*
>>>*my soul straying*

>*according to its law . . .*
>*longing*

>*If time allows*
>*. . . . . or the dream*

acceptance of trespass evolving—

    Suddenly come to an end
    . . .

    My heart insisting . . .

    In exile rising up . . .

    . . .

    The waters of the bitter broom
    you draw down

    The sons and fathers I said I loved . . .
    Free my heart . . .
    so you'll recall —

illness that heals; the notion of kingdom,
and how what pleases could cause such pain

    I asked my soul . . .
    now

    to seal the breach
    and heal each wound . . .

so wisdom and pleasure in time would be one

    and knocking on your door

    I have been judged . . .

    For I've despised
    in the city . . .

For grief and failing,
and ruin in Zion . . .
. . . .

to draw near
. . . struck
clothed in justice—
—listening . . .

how language's lightning in the sentence is won . . .

the two dependent

and how I feel driest watching the rain

a man responding
in despair, calling
softly, thirsty—

with brandy in a glass beside me;

as he chooses
between the walls at noon
. . . .

but not now, as my mind ranges
back over silence's changes—

mercy

and leaves me wondering just how we see

by heart—

and so I start to write these
petitions of a morning's
sighs, and cries for Zion

how what is smallest could loom so large,
how what is best could miss what is finest

     . . . .
Wandering as every wolf pursued me
    it says in ink
from the twelfth century—
straying as every pain came through me

You made hearts glad with what you've done,
    . . . .
splitting the light and extending the heavens
    . . . .
and after forming masses of land,
bringing bread forth from them

and how what is fine

                      and wine

     could be crushed by a blindness

Tell me, what is man
if not dirt and a worm,

    his life is only vapor . . .

caused by a brightness

Tell me what man is
but flesh and blood that's warm,

        reaching the margins

of what it is

    whose life is only vapor . . .

we most attend to——

Tell me, what is man
who knows not whence he comes,

which matters least

his life is only vapor . . .

Tell me what man is,
asleep within his home

and so
his life is only vapor . . .

Tell me——
                    I've grumbled

what is man

searching for what I need

whose heart cannot be known,
whose life is
                    in the rubble

only vapor . . .

. . . of what we've known was true.

These are things on which I've stumbled.

AND SO THE SKIN . . .

And so their pounded hearts
were worn—
                    like a badge
          or talisman
that canceled
almost all their blindness—

creation's linkage depending
                    on a drive itself
   derived from a kind of kindness
or desperation, the sense that one's
inadequate,
                    at any rate

the space for time—

water has it, flowing
(even from a faucet . . .)
and here the black swan glides across it—

as the sunlight's suddenly on my back,
and now the skin along it's warmer,
Lord,
          which lets me walk by the river. . . .

II

NOTES ON BEWILDERMENT

I.

Translation aspires, clearly, beyond its words,
beyond what it renders, beyond even—if through—
sense, yielding, or wielding, blunders and wonder,
erasing our notion of a sacred uniqueness
(the original), as incarnation of what it heard.

II.

Losing one's sense of just where one is one,
and gaining all that in a sense was lost;
confusion's limbo lingers, echoing that
single aspect pinning us down, until
the elusive many is (almost) won.

III.

Verse returns us, although it's fair to ask (it?)—
to what? The cresting wave of recurrence itself?
Essential enfolding? Or just the artifice of
a controlling author? One partakes of infinity;
the other is shut within perfection's casket.

IV.

And how in fact is that return embodied?
Only by means of convention's employment?
Some insist it's through a serial sprawl.
Though one's as fraudulent as the other.
Be careful, then, before deploying your need.

V.

Love is caught in this revolving door
as well, or maybe that should read: "evolving."
Eros draws us back into its swirl,
and somehow we're propelled further into
the world by its spell, which we'd been waiting for.

VI.

I doubt it, he said, the words drawing them down
into an abyss of . . . And that's just it,
the endlessness (as in eternity, dark
as it, in this particular case, may be)
sharing a lot with a divine pronoun.

VII.

Perhaps personal. But who's keeping track?
A woman suggests her Asian discipline implies
it's no one. Not, at any rate, an individual.
Just the wafting of something or other eternal.
Which I believe in, despite my aching back.

VIII.

In the cheap seats. And the executive suite.
Which is to say, my own slug-like conscience,
moving along by, it seems, contracting
against itself. The slime and motion inching me
toward the sublime, through confusion, like wheat.

IX.

Where are you, calls the Lord, from beyond
language, to those who might well answer him,
and thus be said to be alone with God,
as opposed to one who's deaf to the question,
which then becomes: Where *were* you? As everyone's bond.

X.

The flaming sword at Eden's entrance turns
round, every which way, Scripture announces
barring Adam from that garden: Ambivalence,
notes the Rabbi, is the propeller driving us
into the longing no one ever unlearns.

XI.

Any resemblance to actual people or scenes
depicted here is entirely coincidental,
says the disclaimer in the poetry magazine.
The Gazan room, for instance, in which the sleeping
family is crushed by Israelis, beneath their dreams.

XII.

Or, memory's horror: into the rush
of Jews, the bomb's extending toward the opening
doors to the bus——the flash and thunder erasing
skinny Anna, who'd given peace and poetry
the best of her seemingly never-ending lust.

XIII.

It *is* possible, the language itself insists,
or seems to: the poetry *can* come through, though only
by means of indirection. Bad translation
is like drawing a bucket from a moonlit
well——and losing the silvery shine on its surface.

XIV.

It was a golden time, said Rothko,
*for then we had nothing to lose, and a vision
to gain.* Thinking of his youthful loneness,
he wished the graduating class, not success,
but *pockets of silence* in which to *root and grow.*

XV.

Their lines like prongs, raking the shore inside
oneself to coax out what might be of worth
in a world beyond that self. To other
selves and selflessness. There is a power
rinsing spirit with detritus, like a tide.

XVI.

The obsession, with what it means to be a Jew
at heart, the bull's eye with which I began
my thinking, away from and then toward what I am—
may have occluded, although I doubt it,
much of living I've also known was true.

XVII.

That, for instance, what one lovingly does
is passed over with little understanding,
or worse—rewarded with betrayal's hearse,
surely's taken (somewhere) up by Scripture,
reminding us that *will be* of course means *was.*

XVIII.

Always, wrote Machado, *seek in the mirror
the one who's walking beside you, the other*—
though what he meant by that mirror I've never
been sure. Clearly he meant it more than literally,
given his feel for the flowing river.

XIX.

The song, another poet sang, *has gone
out of me,* glossing—theatrically—his loss
of innocence. I, innocent, thought it
the height of profundity. Now I think his
notion of song itself may have done him in.

XX.

The dream of the poem, he told the closest angel
of poetry, asked how he'd titled his book.
The dream of the poem, the warm angel echoed,
adding, bemused: *It's a little weird*—
(which it was) summoning fate, like peril.

XXI.
Singing again of his lady he'd slip
into a vision of the beloved beyond
form, and his fear, and soon he was in His
thrall, forever, a man whose love of the Lord
lay between belief and his knowledge's lip.

XXII.
He wanted to know how love was rewarded:
True Love. That's easy, the lover replied,
the prize for that great desire comprises
the absence of any distinction between
the pain and pleasure one is accorded.

XXIII.
"Terrific," said the reader, his eyebrows
arching, the words' light passing beneath them,
"another *phantasticus*—just what we need,"
although the ideal to be pursued was *real*
as the world that pursuit itself endows.

XXIV.
It isn't done with tracing paper. Things
signaled by words charged in a row begin
to converge, just as hope a single one
or pair might be rendered fades. So we enter
the sacred order from which translation springs.

XXV.
The bereaved speakers droned on and on about
"humanity," entitled by their grief.
Not having to suspend anything in
the way of disbelief, I sat listening
but left with the faint hope I'd brought in doubt.

XXVI.
I don't really get Spinoza, he said,
having, again, tried to enter the *Ethics*.
Ax. Descartes detests the senses' indenture.
Schol. The geometric method's torture.
Cor. The book went back to the shelf unread.

XXVII.
The heart flutters, flitting about between
the past and future notion of things, wavering.
Who would catch it and calm it down, that it
in time might grow still, and, by degrees,
grasp the glory that lasts but is rarely seen?

XXIII.
Augustine. *In the eternal moment,*
he wrote, *nothing passes away; the whole*
is present, though no time is wholly so.
Both future and past are formed and issue
from that (that *what?*) *which is always present.*

XXIX.
Next to the *Zohar,* that mostly obscure
glossary of light, aglow with pleasure
implicating eternity, the normal
mysticism of clear words in a row
moves me more, I confess, and also cures.

XXX.
(In its way. Which is to say, its manner.
which is to say what one means to say,
in as much as that's ever possible,
while not ignoring style's tensile ladder—
though now we're circling back again toward Splendor.)

XXXI.
In an extension of the mind, nearing its
limits—deltas of twisting branches forking
finely towards a pewter sky, shifting as
roots of those trees descend through silt, to sewage
and clay. There, Solomon said, are spirits.

XXXII.
Ethical practice, apart from any quirk
of personal fate, such as, say, religion,
with faith at its core, needs no temple or shrine.
But theology, too, lines that axis,
often as response to what doesn't work.

XXXIII.
What, the lover was asked by his friends, does
happiness mean? He, here, seems to stand for
the writer himself, or maybe the reader
in a dream, or on an off day. *It means,*
he said, *unhappiness borne for what one loves.*

XXXIV.
The postcard from Theresienstadt bore a stamp
of serious interest to the boy, whose
grandmother's message read: *I am in good*
health; everything is fine. "It must," he thought,
"be a nice place for vacation, or a camp."

XXXV.
The dervishes turn on axes as old
as earth's, but pointing toward their own tombstones.
Within their shroud-like cloaks and skirts they spin.
I'd gone thinking I'd see a hackneyed thing,
then watched my heart's arms like their dance unfold.

XXXVI.

Albers' late homages squared no circle.
He pushed green (with orange?) so it seemed red.
He placed a teal form within a gray one.
Or was that *over?* In his Bauhaus head
the absolute was, always, relational.

XXXVII.

What good is thinking that one keeps within?
What value does it have, until it finds
expression, until it bodies forth as
action, events informing work and feeling—
as wisdom is joined to pleasure once again?

XXXVIII.

As in their action selves in relation
are changed, and identities shifted or lost,
so the world is reconfigured, though not,
of course, sensationally. The adjustments
are small, like stills combined in animation.

XXXIX.

Well-housed, salaried, insured, and bourgeois,
like his peers, in a respectable fashion,
Professor X is making, well, a living
around the world for himself with his teaching
the quiet ecstasies of kabblablah.

XL.

All the rivers—it's getting somehow truer
and truer—run into the sea which is
never full, said Kohelet, the preacher,
combining, in lines as close to a sigh
as any might be, pointlessness and splendor.

XLI.
Listen, happiness is a reflection, he said.
It doesn't arise through self-contemplation,
except as that withdrawal deflects one's
recall, like clouds in a skyscraper's glass.
It's a seam, along which the heart is fed.

XLII.
Seeking truth, seek definition and place
your words with care, unless you'd find yourself
ensnared, as a songbird faces twigs smeared
with lime in its own nest. The more it resists them,
the more they stick to it, negating its grace.

XLIII.
Thus the call for clarity. The lovers' creed.
Things heard as though within one. But suddenly
freed by others' words. Nothing's original.
Not even sin. The mild wind now blowing
may be wisdom, bringing someone what he needs.

XLIV.
Bringing him back to the perpetual lie
of freedom in beginning, which is only
freedom to begin. Again. "Art," the poet
said, "it cures affliction," with deception,
even as death endures. Still, we try.

XLV.
If not like Daedalus building those wings
for his son to fly away with, then like
someone telling their story, and killing time,
in a manner of speaking, within that myth's
labyrinth one is always escaping.

XLVI.
Lord, goes the prayer, increase my bewilderment,
which really means allow me to question
everything, but not be lost within that
stance to the small flowers of common sense
in season. Increase, Lord, my discontent.

XLVII.
But keep me from resentment. Reason as well
has its season, although we don't believe it,
or put too much faith in it. It's true that
one and one, on occasion, is three or more.
And the middle way *is* often mystical.

XLVIII.
Lord, goes the prayer, keep me from delusion.
Which really means allow my mind to open
to all that comes my way, without bringing
ruin upon me—through fusion of things that are
distinct at heart. Keep me from conclusion.

XLIX.
While the case is being made. And the world
is all that is the case. Keep me from too much
seclusion. Increase my confusion with
Thee, it says. But is that in fact another
matter, I wondered, as the dervishes whirled?

L.
And may my love and language lead me into
that perplexity, and that simplicity,
altering what I might otherwise be.
But let it happen through speech's clarity—
as normal magic, which certain words renew.

III

THE GHAZAL OF WHAT HE SEES

"If one asks, what is the Depth of Primordial
Being, the answer is: 'Nothing.'"
— Yosef Gikatilla

What he sees when he sees—the wintered almond trees unfolding
white flames of nutrition's pistils through the blueness beckoning—

is nothing without the mind's holding it there in the day's crucible
                                            reckoning;
and when he considers it, that thought, too, is nothing

without the fed fire of the word's burning
into the black whole of knowing's nothing.

It's all a matter of poise in pain, or bliss: an equilibrium.
So words are uttered and sentences made, which are nothing

but a pact arrived at, a living—
a kind of suspension bridge across an infinitely wide, magisterial
                                        river's flotsam flowing,

cables strung and girders soaring,
as though its immeasurable mass, and freight, were nothing.

PALESTINE: A SESTINA

Hackles are raised at the mere mention of Palestine,
let alone The Question of—who owns the pain?
Often it seems the real victims here are the hills—
those pulsing ridges, whose folds and tender fuzz of green
kill with softness. On earth, it's true, we're only guests,
but people live in places, and stake out claims to land.

From Moab Moses saw, long ago—a land
far off, and once I stood there facing Palestine
with Hassan, whose family lives in Amman. (We were his guests
in the Wahdat refugee camp.) Wonder shot with pain
came into his eyes as he gazed across the green
valley between Nebo and Lydda beyond the hills.

Help would come, says the Psalmist, from one of those hills,
though scholars still don't know for certain whether the land
in question was Zion, or the high places of Baal. The green
olives ripened, and ripen, either way in Palestine,
and the memory of groves cut down brings on pain
for those whose people worked them, for themselves or guests.

"I have been made a stranger in my home by guests,"
says Job, in a Hebrew that evolved along these hills,
though he himself was foreign to them. His famous pain
is also that of those who call the Promised Land
home in another tongue. Could what was pledged be Palestine?
Is Scripture's fence intended to guard this mountain's green?

Many have roamed its slopes and fields, dressed in green
fatigues, unable to fathom what they mean, as guests.
And armies patrol still, throughout Palestine,
as ministers mandate women and men to carve up its hills
to keep them from ever again becoming enemy land.
The search, meanwhile, goes on—for a balm to end the pain,

though it seems only to widen the rippling circles of pain,
as though the land itself became the ripples, and its green
a kind of sigh. So spring comes round again to the land,
as echoes cry: "It's mine!"—and the planes will bring in guests,
so long as water and longing run through these hills,
which some (and coins) call Israel, and others Palestine.

The pundits' talk of Palestine doesn't account for the pain—
or the bone-white hills, breaking the heart as they go green
before the souls of guests-on-earth who've known this land.

COEXISTENCE:
A LOST AND ALMOST FOUND POEM

And the Levites shall speak, and say
unto all the men of Israel, with a loud voice:

Over the border the barrier winds,
devouring orchards of various kinds.

Cursed be he that taketh away
    the landmark of his neighbor.
And all the people shall say, Amen.

The road was blocked in a battle of wills—
as the lame and sightless trudged through the hills.

Cursed be he that maketh the blind
    to go astray in the way.
And all the people shall say, Amen.

The army has nearly written a poem:
You'll now need a permit just to stay home.

Cursed be he that perverteth the justice
    due to the stranger (in Scripture).
And all the people shall say, Amen.

Taken away—in the dead of night—
by the secret policeman, who might be a Levite.

Cursed be he that turneth to smite
    his neighbor in secret murder.
And all the people shall say, Amen—

as peace is sought through depredation,
living together in separation.

Cursed be he that confirmeth not
*   the words of this law——to do them.*
And all the people shall say, Amen.

ISRAEL IS

Israel is he, or she, who wrestles
with God—call him what you will,

not some goon (with a rabbi and gun)
in a pre-fab home on a biblical hill.

PROVERBIAL DRAWING

"This world is like a ladder, one descends by it and another ascends."
— Midrash Rabbah, Ruth

I. HOW FAR

How far should he reach—
   the line extends—knowing
it's far from a sound approach,
   rung by abstract rung to heaven?

And where in relation to here
   is *there?* Cut off? Is that right?
Or maybe it's light he's after,
   or only a view—height

and distance from threats below,
   which the ladder offers.
No! It's all in the picture,
   which this one echoes:

"I want, I want," said Blake.
"I can't, I can't," said the fake.

II. A RIGHT ANGLE SUPPORTS US HERE

I don't understand. This cloud
   which should rise hangs
heavy and hovers. This leaded
   whiteness mingles,

disperses dark and summons
   at the same time the same.
There's trouble there, but a platform
   of sorts as well. You came

for a view of the cloud.
   OK. Weather the storm.

III. THE LINE

This is harder, lower,
  both more resolute and remote.
Nothing in the way of help here.
  And so your spirit

floats there between . . . what?
  Always between . . . That's it.
That's how it is: not quite
  a jutting out as a fit-

ting awkwardly in.
  Unavoidable. Usually
invisible. A not so fine
  line inserted—see

it?—in everyone's air—always—
  everywhere.

IV. IT'S TRUE

It's true but funny.
Time is honey.

V. THE HOUSE THE CLOUD

In a desert a dwelling—
   in the dwelling a desert?—
an encampment (an end to wandering),
   a cloud's shade before it,

by night a fire, and from it
   stories emerged. The dwelling itself
had angles, and order, and a pitch
   to its symmetry: There were books and shelves

of a kind, and when things were good,
   it seemed there was more
air within than without. The cloud
   held, it would hover,

for what sometimes felt like forever,
   and they'd forget. But then it would lift,
and again they would wander, and remember.
   Such was the house, the cloud, the gift.

Once upon a time, there was a skyhook
   that didn't quite exist.
It was the stuff of legend, not of a book,
    but frequently told, to trick us,

and others like us, when we were kids.
   Suspended, somehow, from above,
it would lift our tent up over our heads,
   creating a perfect complex peak: a roof.

Then it could be removed.
   What it would hang from, we didn't know,
or try to. But the notion compelled . . .
   and so we were sent off, usually in pairs, to go

from camp to camp and ask if we could borrow
   their skyhook. The man in charge always knew
how to answer: We lent ours out.
   It's two camps down, half-a-mile or so through

those woods. He'd point, and we'd trudge on, grumbling,
   in search of that wondrous device,
the last word in wilderness dwelling,
   which would make for us that immaculate crease

and yield, over our heads, a prize ceiling—
   that weightless, matchless, unnerving and skyey,
legend-like feeling of being,
   at last, held up from on high.

(VALENT)LINES FOR A.

What law and power has blessed me so
that in this provocation of flesh
    I have been wedded to gentleness?

*

Delicacy of an intricate
mesh of our thought and meals and talking
    has brought me to this exaltation

of syllables and a speechlessness—
to December dusk, and desk, and skin
    in the amber of our listening.

*

Dawn again pink with munificence;
heart again blurred by its ignorance:
    toward you in that equation I turn—

and you, in turn, involve our being
spun like wool from which soul is weaving
    a use for that useless opulence.

*

Doing and making—the end served by
what it is we make, and what we do,
    is what has made me: making and you.

SUFI ABSTRACTS

after Ibn Arabi, et al.

I.
He who seeks God
    and turns to his mind
in confusion is quartered
    by the Lord he would find.

II.
If I'm present I don't see a thing
    when I look—for it's enough
        that he, unseen and all-seeing,
directs me: "I," it's said, is an obstacle.

And if I'm absent, in mystery's strangeness,
    my absence in absence ranges
        far and wide—its evident
radiance—his—yours—immutable . . .

III.
Your splendor is all my heart craves,
and it holds my mind
        in its spell without fail.

Your gaze for me is an abstract jail,
    release from which
makes of my friends' faces graves.

IV.
The thought of you comes and I die—
    and then I revive;
and thus it is I've died so often
    I've lived ten thousand lives.

WHY DOES THE WORLD OUT THERE SEEM

1.

Why does the natural feel unnatural?
Why does the world out there seem
so utterly foreign to these poems?
It isn't strange, and hardly hostile,
to the heart and eye behind their lines:
dirt exploding into spring,
leaves climbing the pipe to the screen,
the morning glory's funnel of blue,
the sap of it all coursing through
every fiber of all those veins.
Why does the natural feel so strained
when set beside the abstract figures
of speech's discourse linking us?
Poems, as Williams wrote, are machines.

2.

But maybe the natural's not what I mean,
so much as experience *of* the natural
merged with that which men have made.
No, not that. It's registration
of things one feels have already been
established as facts by the eyes and mind.
Once is plenty. And that's the sacred.
Why the need to return to the scene
of each epiphany? Why the craving
for that halo? A kind of greed?
Natural lines on a piece of paper
are revelation enough for now,
as are speaking and listening to
you and what these words might say.

3.

Extending beyond information, but also
observation of that natural
world which observation reveals
as a miracle. Or not beyond—
beside. Maybe even beneath.
Or breached. That's the thread leading
back and possibly out or through:
to what or whom? Him? You?
I'm here, almost against my will,
having been led, as though by the nose,
by language. And in this abstract picture
I'm asking you to bear with me.
Reader. Readers. Reading. We
are in this instant's chain together.

4.

A chain partaking of enchantment,
mystics have written, implying song,
and maybe the poem. Or just a spell.
Which might as easily be a hell-
ish hall of echoes or mirrored images
mixing in the hungry mind.
Or, diversion which doesn't feed
and draws one further from, not toward,
the pool of pleasure wisdom is.
Depending on the poem's design.
Strange how I've become a modern
poet of a medieval kind—
making poems for a different diversion,
as they point toward what's divine.

5.

Amusement derives from the animal's mouth
and snout, stuck there in the air,
as it stares, struck by words
it heard. In a manner of speaking
it muzzles as in what's not fair,
or wonder. And in the illogical moment
of what it means and how it works,
while the mouth is closed, nourishment—
if it's serious—enters through it.
And in a nutshell that's the sentence
and solace that sweet Chaucer meant.
The poem's gesture, changing, survives
in generations of aspiration,
leading us on . . . or into our lives.

THE MEANING OF

What is the meaning of Then?

Not now. I'm busy—
can't you see—with
weaning Now from what
was then. Alright,
but when will you have Time

again for the meaning of Then?

I repeat, not
yet. . . . Soon . . . I'll turn
to Then, and Then itself
will maybe leave us
meaning we might glean

from "What is the meaning of Then?"

For now it gives Now meaning
and keeps it from simply falling
into an abyss of
When. . . . And what could we
do then? Now, listen:

What is the meaning of Then?

Is it a consummation?
Or merely an expectation?
Or only a defense
against disintegration?
Does it imply salvation?

What *is* the meaning of Then?

And is there a single solution?
Is it a cause for mourning?
How long have you been longing?
And might it involve celebration
of a Now that's bound to Then?

Is *this* the meaning of Then?

How does humiliation
figure in this equation?
Has it become an ideal
held up for reflection?
And where in this is perfection?

Does the meaning of Then

function as an icon?
Could it move us a micron
closer to restitution?
But what of that explosion
after Then's implosion?

What is the meaning of Then

for the heart and for compassion,
concretion and abstraction?
Is it simply a part
of the history of illusion?
It does help with confusion.

Is there a meaning of Then

without all this confusion?
Must it emerge from penance,
or some existential disturbance
to the self and soul as one?
And again we come to the sentence:

"What is the meaning of Then?"

as though I'd just awoken
to an essential discord.
It makes the needle of the mind
skip as over an old record
which, it seems, is broken:

What is the meaning of Then?

What is the meaning of Then?

What is the meaning of Then?

LINES FOR A SLIM COLLECTED POEMS

in memory of Avraham Ben Yitzhak

He hoped it would happen just when it would,
when the spirit listeth, and it listed not;

and worth was all in inclusive resistance:
the perfect silence of the polyglot.

From THE NECESSITY OF WHAT ISN'T NECESSARY

after al-Ma'arri, 11th century

You stand there as the driven
    wheels of heaven spin—
and choose,
    while the fates are laughing.

HOMAGE TO AGNES

Now I am spinning and turn
to her of the mild mind
     whose lines extend
quietly out from God-knows-where
and into the picture we see in color
before us,
       however pale.
The lines continue
from that square and into the world
we sometimes notice
when we're there—
the thinnest of reddish filaments
like a band-aid's string
running through it,
or calming strips of manila and beige.

Its grid, it seems to me, is true,
and her straightest lines amaze.

THE RAIN

The rain coming down in winter
when I was younger—
say by twenty years—hit the stones
in what seemed then like a sexual manner,
as though its cold ran through my bones.

Now, the room is warmer,
and my bones, too, are no longer
what they were—or even, in places, my own.
The inner seems both less and more
within, and the moments are hours

in which what was and is is sewn.

SOMETHING MORE

I hadn't noticed for a decade and then
there it was, soaring—
the date-palm like an asterisk
   high in the pale-blue powdery air
over the walls of the centuries' city,

implying a kind of (long-lost) commentary
beneath the print of that day's page
or tucked at the back of a certain chapter,
   if one would ever get there.
But what (in the world) was it trying to say,

I wondered. For it wouldn't go away
long after I'd left it behind,
and wandered home. It floated still
   inside my thinking, as though
that, too, were that thing

bespeaking both itself
and something more, to come,
and which had just been before.
   Such was life with an asterisk,
hovering over it like a palm.

IV

WHAT HAS BEEN PREPARED

1.

The eye, it seems, hath not seen
what has been prepared
for him that waiteth *for him*——

What is the meaning of *been prepared?*

That which the I
                    has not seen
drifting out from the garden

beyond the eye as it's feeding feeling:

the wine of the word to come
        and the sweetness it pours forth.

The face of a friend or the foreign.

Disappointing or transporting.

What has been prepared
        before the eye could see
    in Scripture is known as Eden
    or the garden's
        blessing beyond its first person——

    which is work that *waiteth for him.*

*

What is the meaning of *waiteth for him?*

Breathing.

The azure air inspired,

the bilious self-sorrow strained,

the rotting stasis of the mimetic

(or a moral end achieved)

but not any irritable reaching
    after the easy image or scene—

. . .

the classical cool and world
needing neither motion or comment
                appeals—

but the untroubled classical mind's not mine:

mine is always leaning
      into a certain wind
   from when
or where I'm not quite sure—

though everything seems to be in it—

and the wind itself a leaning

—at heart the dis-
   quiet and quest

the un-
satisfied nature of sense . . .

Which seems to me like a listening

to what has come before
through what has not yet been.

Irritation, then, as transgression
only for the placid spirit,
        the pearl-less soul—

reaching isn't arriving,

translation is never ending

—the distance between *adore* and *adorn*

or asking
what our hearing means.

*

Sounds of rain in the trees and leaves, or a sinking feeling with the water running. In the kitchen. Kestrels screeching. Jackdaws squawking. Overhead, just now, a plane. A tourist asking directions. A spouse expressing discontent. A president trying to form a sentence. A radio host from Monte Carlo. The heavenly host from a poem's refrain. A muffled rumble behind the day: a low haze of cloudy cover. Skin slid on a cotton sheet. A pencil's lead across the paper. Things we own and things we don't. Things we know. A home creaking. Blood boiling. A neighbor's door suddenly opening. The sound of the rain giving way to snow.

II. WHAT DOES ALWAYS MEAN

A revelation forgotten:
the bread of proposition
set before him *always,*
as a holy portion,

as a perpetual debt
to him within creation.
What does always mean
in Israel's instigation?

Does it recognize hunger
among the other nations,
let alone its own?
Or does its singular station

excuse it now in time?
This bread which has been called
the bread of faces faces—
said Ibn Ezra—God

facing men and women
facing women and men.
A revelation forgotten.
The bread of prepositions—

of souls and objects in
relation. *And then the priests*
entered bearing bread:
for the hungry, a feast

within that sanctuary
of what is written, and wrung
into and out of hours.
And they will be known among

the nations. Justice will be
their diversion—a presence
leading up from the mouth
of malice, which has no defense

without it. And so the pact
was kept at the tent of meeting's
table. And Johanan said:
Great is the act of eating.

*

Always an eye for the morsel. Often a lick of the local lokum, its fauna and flora. A well-cut brick. Or sky—out an open window. Always a meal deduced from the raw—reconfigured by heat or hurt, or ice's application. Always an eye for the hesitation, an inclination, the national debt. Glasses a loved one's about to forget. Always a moral. Always a plate and always motion. Always the politician's contortion. Always a lie in the eye toward spin. Or giving something away for nothing. Often a burnt offering and no-tion. Always the teaching and instruction. Always the law and all it weighs. (Often the haze, for days.) Sometimes it pays. Always the priestly portion.

III. WHAT INTIMATION IS THERE

Their habitation shall be appalled
—says the prophet.

What intimation is there that

their habitation shall be appalled
to them
        means

anything other than what it seems?

Or that *the least*
    of the flock shall drag them away

(which is glossed in Scripture as
either Greece or Persia

within our, always, lives)

isn't in our minds
or waiting at their borders?

Their refers to Edom—
Rome within the Rabbis' teaching,

but who now is Rome's vassal,

and what has been destroyed
within its habitation?

Your horror has deceived you;
even pride within your heart.

And who here has been appalled?

The swine holds up its parted hooves
as it brings destruction on
(in the Rabbis' teaching),
    as if to say:
    I am pure

and prove its moral standing.

And so the twisted kingdom
as it wreaks its havoc
    looks as though it has
convened a higher court of justice.

Its lawyers tell the world it's clean.

*

*Making the empty desert bloom. Virgin soil. Although we need just a little
more room. All that oil; all those countries. A narrow waist was once its pride.
Now it's wide and the world's against it. Nothing upsets it. Not apartheid
in its midst, not its lies, not the fence. Cutting the land like a local Christo.
It takes a village. Along the ridge. From whence, says Scripture, cometh my
help. Slowly but surely. Ethnic cleansing? Must stay strong. As you see, we've
done nothing wrong . . . that we weren't forced to. (We only do what we have to
do.) We're like you: Everything we say is true. Though nothing living along
this seam is, in fact, what it seems. If you will it, said the prophet, it is no
dream.*

*Making the desert empty. Bloom, purging soil. As though it needed a little
more room. All that toil, come from countries: "Waste not, want not" once its
pride. Now its eyes for the world are wide. And nothing it does upsets us.
There's no apartheid in its midst. That's no lie, we need the fence . . . Wander-
ing through the land like Christ. Take that village along the ridge. Who on
earth could bring it help? Ethnic cleansing, Scripture says. Slowly but surely.
Staying strong is hardly wrong; our forces do what must be done. Nothing
that they do is fun. Living along this seam. Where is, in fact, is what it seems.
If you will it, said the prophet. It is not a dream.*

IV. WHAT THEN IS APPEASED

God will judge
    when one man sins
        against another—
say the sages
    in the Mishna,
        but later explain:
Transgressions against another man
    first must be appeased by him
        (before God can forgive).

What *did* the sages believe?
Could God be less than a person
    who's been oppressed or aggrieved?
Does divine judgment depend on man?

Or maybe He's the power behind
    what's given to be appeased
in the case of transgression against a person,
    or people—so that the appeasement receives
        its share of that power as will?

Appeasement begins with another's honor
which is at once one's own:
and failure to honor the other
involves a diminishment of what one knows
    of that honor deriving
        from what the sages call The Place,
            or in translation, The Omnipresent—

All that is seen and known within

the place of the grudge or in forgiving
    relation to a face—
    whether another's or one's own.

The Midrash affirms that the crime
of extermination begins
before murders have taken place—

goes the survivor-philosopher's thinking,

oppression and uprooting
(of the law of house and home)
already signal its beginnings. . . .

And then he summons the Sages'
David through quotation:

Only the merciful, humble, and they
who perform acts of benevolence
    are fit to be part of this nation.

*

Bordering being and ordering skin. Quartering faith and water for drinking, crops and bathing. Lights and nations. What's kept out and what's let in. A kind of equation: As without, so within. A single law . . . for stranger and citizen? Who's who kidding? Where's that mirror? As we've done unto others. Once again. That All is seen and known within. Trace of the grudge and of forgiving. As the wind picks up with evening. On the island no one is.

V. WHAT IS IT THAT GIVES RISE

An ear open, as though a funnel
to words preserved by those who've told us:
I am only ashes and dust;
I am a worm and not a man;

and Moses' asking before the Lord,
What are *we?* which the rabbis heard
as *We are nothing,* and then explained:
Over nothing He hangs the world.

*

What is it that gives rise to this?
How does their vision of the ear emerge
or Sages' understanding of selves?
The listening which is Scripture's premise?

To rub its words as though extracting
juice from fruit or the spirit that shaped them?
Or Rava buried in study, distracted,
rubbing his foot and leaving a wound?

Or so to blow on the ashes one finds
until, with breath, they start to glow . . .
This too has been prepared,
and as above, so below—

Abraham, refusing plunder,
swore that *from a sandal strap*
to a thread, he'd *take not a thing;*
for which he was given the thought of heaven

along with its azure to wrap about him,
as if he were swimming in its sea,
as though he'd said, "As for me,
I am the after-taste of ashes,

I taste the dust of what has been
and *will* be"—though this is far from complacency,
note the sages, or just humility.
This is what, they say, is given

as being's foundation, by which we exist:
Through the merit of men in a quarrel
able to render themselves as nothing—
by this alone, the world subsists . . .

*

Radiant morning funneling blue: into the glow of evening's robes. As though she knew what she wanted to do, or who she'd told. There are, said the kabbalist, two hundred and thirty-one gates in the soul. But did he mean the soul of all——or only Israel? Or maybe the Mind they call Supernal? And gates to what? As doors to where? Make, say the Fathers, a fence for Scripture (of which it's written:"Turn it and turn it, all is in it"). They're making a fence to guard the future . . . of the People, it says in the paper. And it has many gates as well. And they too are in the soul, and of Israel. But gates to where? Doors for whom? Under the glow of evening's robe. And into the radiant morning blue.

VI. WHAT IS MEANT BY BEING

What is meant by being bound?

As one who boards a train?

Or she whose mind is held by something
pulsing in her field of vision,
    or sugar through her veins?

Or bound as in embodied—
spirit fleshed—or just
a personal
            relegation
    to religion's
    being tied
back to what's behind him
and perhaps to come?

Does it mean that one is blind?

Or does one then see further,
and not just what is found
    before one's eyes

even in the lightless night?

Or is it to the present,
as if it were a scent—
in a syntax, but heaven-sent?

(In-
finity's aroma,
the masters of
   reception call it

down from a certain height.

And try to tell us:

   Bound to bless—
with a measure of terror—
with the frankincense of slippage
   and the ambergris of sense,
   the steady flame of bestowal
and the choice words of a spoken sentence

or parts of speech
that are like a tent of meeting—

and meant
       by being bound.

*

Out with only a nose for spring, success's rat or roasting chicken. White viburnum. A municipal mess and the Western wind. Promising land. Almond blossoms over axons, dispersing a sweetness high in the brain. Worms turning beneath the garden. An ethic rotting. Oils brushed-up in my walking: hyssop, sage, anise, thyme. Herbs crushed. Shifting nouns. Canaan. Sion.

CODA

THE GHAZAL OF WHAT HURT

Pain froze you, for years—and fear—leaving scars.
But now, as though miraculously, it seems, here you are

walking easily across the ground, and into town
as though you were floating on air, which in part you are,

or riding a wave of what feels like the world's good will—
though helped along by something foreign and older than you are

and yet much younger too, inside you, and so palpable
an X-ray, you're sure, would show it, within the body you are,

not all that far beneath the skin, and even in
some bones. Making you wonder: Are you what you are—

with all that isn't actually you having flowed
through and settled in you, and made you what you are?

The pain was never replaced, nor was it quite erased.
It's memory now—so you know just how lucky you are.

You didn't always. Were you then? And where's the fear?
Inside your words, like an engine? The car you are?!

Face it, friend, you most exist when you're driven
away, or on—by forms and forces greater than you are.

NOTES

IMPROVISATION ON LINES BY ISAAC THE BLIND

The opening translates lines by Isaac the Blind, a thirteenth-century kabbalist from Provence, in his commentary to the early medieval mystical tract *Sefer Yetzira (The Book of Creation)*.

THINGS ON WHICH I'VE STUMBLED

A *geniza* is a storeroom that holds worn out and discarded Hebrew texts. In Jewish practice, these texts cannot simply be thrown away; because they bear the name of God, they are held until they can be given a ritual burial in accordance with Jewish law. This poem is based on unidentified fragments of eleventh- and twelfth-century Hebrew poems I came across while working at the Genizah Research Unit at the University Library in Cambridge. The Unit contains manuscripts discovered in the late nineteenth century when, as the story is usually told, two Scottish "ladies" (in fact unemployed Assyriologists) purchased fragments of a text from an antiquities dealer in Cairo and brought them back to Solomon Schechter, the Reader in Rabbinics at Cambridge. Schechter recognized them as verses from the long-lost Hebrew original of the apocryphal book of Ecclesiasticus, then known only in translation to Greek and other languages. Understanding the importance of the find, he traveled to Egypt and was led to the *geniza* of an Old Cairo synagogue. This particular *geniza* held not only sacred texts, but documents of all sorts composed in the Hebrew alphabet. For a variety of reasons—including a legend which held that the papers were guarded by a large serpent that lay coiled in the darkness—the items in what has become known as the Cairo Geniza never made it to a ritual burial. Preserved largely intact, they turned out to include hundreds of thousands of poems and documents—everything from personal letters, commercial correspondence, legal contracts, and household inventories to children's primers and shopping lists scribbled on the back of other texts. Schechter purchased the entire cache and brought it back to Cambridge, where it is today.

On the whole, italicized sections of the poem translate passages found there. Many of the fragments come from a part of the collection that the library had nearly burned, thinking it "rubbish" and "nothing of any interest or value," as two of the librarians once put it in their written evaluations of the material.

I.

Rags really: Most of the fragments were written on rag paper made of linen. Some are on vellum.

Keats: "Lines Supposed to Have Been Addressed to Fanny Brawne," which were found in the margin of a page on which Keats had written another work; they were first published some eighty years after his death: "This living hand, now warm and capable . . . here it is—I hold it towards you."

On their sleeves: Geniza records indicate that robes sometimes contained quotations from poems embroidered on their sleeves!

Two women (twins): Mrs. Lewis and Mrs. Gibson, who bought the fragment of Ecclesiasticus.

iron gall: The ink used was more often than not made from iron gall (the gall of an oak tree, mixed with wine and other ingredients).

Do not speak: From Schechter's initial letter to Mrs. Lewis, May 13, 1896.

II.

Eric Gill: The British sculptor/designer/typographer (1882–1940). This book is set in Perpetua, which Gill designed in 1925.

Ibn Khalfon: Generally considered the first "professional" poet of the Spanish-Hebrew middle ages.

V.

Things on which I've stumbled: "When a person accustoms himself to studying the Mystery of Creation . . . it is impossible that he not stumble. It is therefore written (Isaiah 3:6), 'Let these ruins be under your hand' [or 'This stumbling block is under your hand']. This refers to things that a person cannot grasp unless they cause him to stumble." *(Bahir 51)*

THE GHAZAL OF WHAT HE SEES

Yosef Gikatilla: A thirteenth-century kabbalist. The epigraph comes from his *Sha'arei Orah* (Gates of Light), Gate Five.

PALESTINE: A SESTINA

The Question of: As in Edward Said's book *The Question of Palestine,* but not only.

Moab: Site of Mount Nebo, from which Moses saw the Promised Land he could not enter.

Lydda: Now the Israeli town of Lod, site of Ben-Gurion International Airport.

The Psalmist: Psalm 121:1-2. Some readings suggest that the line refers to Yahweh's celestial abode, for which "the Mountain of Zion" is an epithet; others read it as an ironic statement and say it refers to the high places where the baals, the local fertility gods, were worshiped.

Job: Job 19:15.

Scripture's fence: "Make a fence around the Torah" (*The Sayings of the Fathers,* I:1, cf. VI:6).

COEXISTENCE: A LOST AND ALMOST FOUND POEM

The refrain-like stanzas in italics are virtually direct quotes from Deuteronomy 27:17, 18, 19, 24, and 26, respectively. The rhymed couplets gloss standard occurrences in the Occupied Territories, widely reported in the Israeli and international press.

ISRAEL IS

The word *Israel* is, in the Bible, derived from the combination of *yisreh* (he wrestles / struggles) and *El* (god); Jacob is renamed Israel after he wrestles with the angel of God at Peniel (Genesis 323:25ff).

PROVERBIAL DRAWING

I want, I want: The caption to an illustration in Blake's *The Gates of Paradise,* b9.

In the desert a dwelling: Loosely alludes to the pillars of cloud and fire accompanying the Israelites in the desert and sometimes descending before Moses' tent when they rested (Exodus 13:21; 33:9; Numbers 14:4).

SUFI ABSTRACTS

These poems adapt the work of a variety of poets, including Hallaj and Muhyyidin Ibn al-'Arabi, both major figures in the Sufi tradition.

WHY DOES THE WORLD OUT THERE SEEM

Amusement derives: i.e., etymologically. The poem plays with the word's derivation: < MF *amuser* < *à* at (< L *ad*) + OF *muser* to stare; muse < OF *muser* to reflect, loiter; prob. orig,. to stay with the muzzle in the air < OF *mus* animal's mouth.

LINES FOR A SLIM COLLECTED POEMS

Avraham Ben Yitzhak (also known as Abraham Sonne, 1883–1950) is a legend in the history of Hebrew poetry and one of its most admired figures, though his entire oeuvre consists of only eleven published poems. Ben Yitzhak spoke or read German, Yiddish, Hebrew, English, and probably Polish, and had studied some Chinese, for starters. See Avraham Ben Yitzhak, *Collected Poems,* translated by Peter Cole, edited and with an afterword by Hannan Hever (Ibis Editions, 2003).

FROM "THE NECESSITY OF WHAT ISN'T NECESSARY"
al-Ma'arri: Abu al-'Ala al-Ma'arri (973–1058) was one of medieval Arabic's
   major poets and thinkers. He was born and raised in Syria, and was blind
   from an early age.

HOMAGE TO AGNES
The painter Agnes Martin.

WHAT HAS BEEN PREPARED
I.
The eye, it seems . . . : Isaiah 64:3, as it appears in the Talmudic discussion on mes-
   sianism in *Sanhedrin* 99a.
Work: cf. Genesis 2:15.

II.
The showbread is, in Hebrew, *lehem ha-panim,* literally, the bread of faces.
   Cf. Exodus 25:30: "And thou shalt set upon the table [inside the desert
   Sanctuary, or the Tent of Meeting] showbread before me always"; also
   Leviticus 24:9, and *Menahot* 99b-100a.
Ibn Ezra: the medieval Hebrew poet and exegete Avraham Ibn Ezra.
Great is the act of eating: Sanhedrin 103b: "Of great [import] is the mouthful [of
   food and drink] . . . it alienates those who are near and draws near those
   who are distant."
Lokum: Turkish delight.

III.
Greece and Persia: The allusions to these powers are in Daniel 8:20, 21.
Swine: The image of the swine trying to prove its purity and fitness for con-
   sumption because its hooves are cloven, though it does not chew its cud,
   is from the Midrash, *Genesis Rabbah* 65:1, where Edom/Rome is chastised
   for its ability to deceive even the prophets with its sophistication.

IV.
Samuel: in 1 Samuel 2:25.
The Midrash affirms: Yebamot 79b. Emmanuel Levinas (who spent much of WWII
   in a German prisoner-of-war camp) is "the survivor-philosopher." Most of
   his Lithuanian family was killed in the Holocaust.
David: The rabbis have King David say that only those who exhibit these three
   characteristics are fit to join the nation of Israel.

V.

I am only ashes: Spoken by Abraham in his "negotiations" with God at Sodom
(Genesis 18:27).

I am a worm: Spoken by David in Psalms 22:7.

What are we: Spoken by Moses before God in the desert and then before the
people (Exodus 16:8). The Rabbis, in a somewhat complicated play on
the Hebrew, understand it to mean "We are nothing."

Over nothing he hangs the world: Job 26:7.

Rava: A prominent Talmudic sage (d. 352 C.E.). This image appears in *Shabbat*
88a-b.

Abraham refusing plunder: When Abraham rescues Lot and returns to the King
of Sodom what the latter had lost in his war with Chedorlaomer (Genesis
14:23), Abraham refuses to take "so much as the strap of a sandal or a
thread" from that booty and is rewarded by God with two "command-
ments"—one concerning the blue thread that must be woven into the
prayer shawl (Numbers 15:37), and the other concerning the strap on
the phylacteries to be worn during the weekday morning prayers (Exodus
13:1-10, 11–16; Deuteronomy 6:4–9, 11:13–22). For this and the other
rabbinic pronouncements that follow, see *Hullin* 88b.

VI.

Infinity's aroma: from the Zohar's commentary to Leviticus 6: 1ff.

THE GHAZAL OF WHAT HURT

An ode to—among other things—titanium, training, and translation.

PETER COLE is the author of *Rift* and *Hymns & Qualms,* recently reissued as *What Is Doubled: Poems 1981–1998.* His many volumes of translations from Hebrew and Arabic include *The Dream of the Poem: Hebrew Poetry from Muslim and Christian Spain, 950–1492* and *So What: New & Selected Poems* by Taha Muhammad Ali. Cole, who lives in Jerusalem and co-edits Ibis Editions, has received numerous awards for his work, including the PEN Translation Prize for Poetry (for *J'accuse* by Aharon Shabtai, New Directions, 2003), a *TLS* Translation Prize, and fellowships from the NEA, the NEH, and the John Simon Guggenheim Foundation. In 2007 he was named a MacArthur Foundation Fellow.